B. ... CASTLE   Photo: Christine Matthews

Message from Emma, Duchess of Rutland,

Patron of Dayglo Books Ltd.

I am delighted to be the Patron of Dayglo Books Ltd.
As a person with dyslexia myself,
I appreciate these books being available. The people
at Dayglo Books have a real passion for making
reading more accessible than ever before to dyslexic
people. They have foresight and talent and truly
believe in the joy of reading for pleasure.

A

Nottinghamshire

Pitman's Story

David Coleman

To/ Theresa x

D J Coleman

5 - 2 - 20

Dayglo Books

Published by
Dayglo Books Ltd, Nottingham, UK

www.dayglobooks.co.uk

ISBN 978-1-911425-65-6

© David Coleman 2017

Cover artwork & illustrations by

www.valentineart.co.uk

Photography by Victoria White

www.darkroomanddigital.co.uk

Typeset in Opendyslexic

by Abelardo Gonzales (2013)

Printed in England

Distributed by Filament Publishing Ltd

Foreword by Dr David Amos

*"Colman's mustard, Colman's starch, tell
Mr Colman to shove it up his . . . nose!"*

So commences the repertoire of David Coleman,
a historical coalmining entertainer, known locally as
the Eastwood Pitman.

I didn't know David during the time we both
worked in the local deep coalmining industry. I was
at Annesley Colliery, later to become Annesley-
Bentinck. David was initially at Moorgreen Colliery and
later transferred to Thoresby Colliery.

However, our paths were destined to cross in
the world of coalmining heritage. It happened while
I was a Heritage Assistant at the D.H. Lawrence
Museum and Heritage Centre in 2002.

I saw David perform his unique one man historical coalmining show on several occasions. It soon dawned on both of us that we shared a common interest in the promotion of the local coalmining heritage.

Both of us have long family backgrounds in the coalmining industry. This has stood us in good stead for understanding the historical context of coalmining and coal communities in the locality.

We have performed many joint mining-heritage events over the last 15 years. Perhaps the pick of these was the "Requiem for Notts Coal" event in August 2015.

This was a commemoration of the coal industry in Nottinghamshire following the closure of the county's last colliery at Thoresby, near Edwinstowe, on 10th July 2015.

David, Tony Kirby and I, dressed as miners, complete with pit-muck, did the symbolic 'walk home'.[14]

We walked from Brinsley Headstocks to the Breach House, followed by dozens of people. This was the same walk which Arthur Lawrence would have done on many occasions.

Arthur Lawrence was a sub-contractor, or butty as they were known locally. He was the father of the world famous author, D.H. Lawrence.

The event concluded with the Eastwood Male Voice Choir performing a selection of mining themed songs at the D.H. Lawrence Heritage Centre, known locally as Durban House.

It is a great privilege for me to contribute the forward to this book. It is a wonderful initiative, telling the story of coal based on David Coleman's one man show – a history of coalmining through the spoken word, pit-talk, local dialect and all!

Enjoy!

Dr David Amos
Research Assistant in Coal and Dialect
School of Arts and Humanities
Nottingham Trent University

February 2017

A

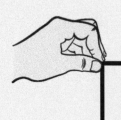

Nottinghamshire

Pitman's Story

1

2

3

Chapter 1

Coleman – it was a good name to work down the pit with, wasn't it? I'm an ex-miner and member of the Mines Rescue Service.[1]

As I'm telling you this story, it's only about a year since the closure of Kellingley pit brought the deep mining of coal to an end in this country.

First I want to say a word about deep mining. You have to understand that 'deep' really does mean what it says.

One of the pits I regularly worked at was as deep as the tallest building in the world is high.

I thought about that recently when I was watching a programme on TV about the Dubai Tower.

That building is half a mile tall. There was
a chap right at the top, with a camera. The view down
to the bottom made your stomach drop.

But then I thought, if you turned that building
up-side down and pushed it into the ground – that is
how deep a miner would be working down in the pit.

It really brought it home to me, in a way that
I hope it will to you, what a very, very long way into
the earth we went down to do our job.

The reason we had to go so far down is
because that is where the coal was. In places there
are what they call 'open cast' mines where the coal
is so near the surface you can see it sitting there. It's
just a matter of digging it out and taking it away by
lorry.

But in other places the coal occurs in layers
– or 'seams' as they are referred to – much further
below the surface.

First of all, when the coal has been located,
a vertical shaft has to be constructed going down to
the level of the coal. 'Roadways', as we call them, are
tunneled out below. That's where the coal is dug out.

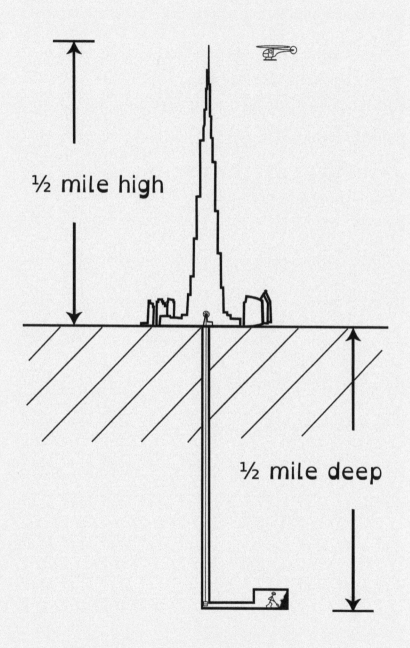

½ mile high

½ mile deep

A lift, known as a 'cage', is used to lower men and machinery down to the bottom of the shaft.

When the coal has been dug out it is moved by one means or another along the roadways to the bottom of the lift shaft, to be hauled to the surface in the cage.

It has always been a dirty, dangerous occupation, but it gave a living to many families for generations.

Chapter 2

The reason for coal being mined commercially is that it burns easily. The burning of coal produces heat. Heat, in turn, is vital to many manufacturing processes. One example is the generation of electricity.

So, what is coal? Coal is the fossilised remains of trees. Living trees contain mostly carbon. Therefore, coal is made up of mostly carbon.

In the distant past, when dinosaurs roamed the earth, there were huge forests of trees. Over time, the trees fell, rotted into the soil and were covered over. They sank down further and further below the surface. The weight above them crushed them flat.

That ancient compacted material is now coal.[4]

Why does coal burn?

We know that coal is made of mostly carbon. Carbon reacts very easily with oxygen.

Oxygen is all around us in the air we breathe. Human beings can't survive without it.

If you put carbon and oxygen together and add a spark, there will be a chain reaction. They will ignite and burn.

Let us say you put coal in the fireplace at home. Oxygen is all around you. You produce a spark with a match or a lighter. The coal will ignite. There is your chain reaction. Your fire will soon be burning and it will produce heat.

Down the pit there has to be oxygen for the miners to breathe. There is also the continual presence of a gas called methane. It is ever-present because it is naturally produced within the coal. It seeps out as the coal is cut and moved about the mine. When methane gas mixes with oxygen and a spark occurs nearby, it explodes.

In a mine a spark can be produced by the friction of a miner's pick striking the coal, or the tools he uses striking a rough stone surface.

So, down the pit you can't avoid the oxygen because it is what the miners need to breathe. You can't avoid the carbon because that is the very stuff the coal is made of. And you can't avoid the methane gas because it is in the coal.

So what you hope to avoid is the methane gas, the carbon and the oxygen coming together, with an unexpected spark causing an explosion and setting fire to the coal.

When nobody causes a spark, the oxygen, carbon and methane gas co-exist quite happily in the pit. It is a spark caused by working activity that can set off an explosion and create a fire.

Think of this scenario. You use a match to set a coal fire burning in the fireplace at home. You have a nice cosy blaze to sit round. Everything is well controlled.

But now think of this scenario. Underground, you have a mixture of carbon, oxygen and methane gas together near the coal face. If they combine and a spark sets them alight, you won't be cosy for long.

You will be running for your life because they will explode.

There are not many industries where men are put at so much risk as they are in coal mining. Health and safety have to be taken very seriously.

The gasses underground are lethal because you can't see them and you can't smell them. You can walk into them, totally unaware.

Chapter 3

In Victorian times, the pit owners built a lot of houses exclusively for the miners.

The 'coal getter' of the family was the only person entitled to rent one of these houses. That was the only way a family could live there.

That is why they always hoped for sons. So if anything happened to the man of the house, the boy could go down the pit and become the 'coal getter'.

Then the family wouldn't be turned out of the house. The pit owners wanted somebody in every one of their houses that would get coal.

In a family where there were only girls in the house, it was a sad story. If the father got killed, with no son to follow him, the pit owners wouldn't care tuppence about evicting the family. If the family wouldn't leave, they would send round the bailiffs and forcibly put them out on the street. Then, next day somebody else would move in, who was a man, with sons.

THE PRICE OF COAL

A roof fall takes you prisoner,
Coal can break your bones,
Dust can clog your lungs,
But only people make you cry.
Scars across my back,
Sweat runs in my eyes.
I take many risks,
Work with little light.
The flame from my candle
Can ignite methane gas.
If the blast doesn't get you
After-damp surely will.
The price of coal is high.
Widows tell the truth.
Owners count their profits,
That's what makes you sigh.

If you go round mining areas you see rows and rows of terraced houses – more than forty houses sometimes in one long terrace.

When the rent man came calling, the family in the first house used to knock on the wall of the house next door. By the time the rent man had got to about number 17, everybody knew the rent man was on his way to them!

Then, if they hadn't got the money to pay, they wouldn't answer the door when he knocked. They would pull the curtains and sit as quiet as mice until he gave up and went away.

Large families were common then, so girls often stayed at home with their mother to help look after the other children.

Boys often followed their fathers and older brothers into a trade.

It would depend on where they lived, as to what that trade might be. In some places they might go to work in a mill, or a brewery, or a brick works, or a ship-yard. At the coast there would be fishing boats.

Wherever there was coal mining, nearly every young lad worked down the pit.

Chapter 4

Now I'm going to tell you something about working life in the early 1900s.

The school leaving age was eleven years old. That's right – only as far as the end of junior school nowadays. It was not until 1918 that the school leaving age went up to fourteen.

So, until the end of the First World War, boys went out to work from the age of eleven or twelve.

So, imagine this: The year is 1902. The man of the house comes up from the pit. He's all dirty and he's fed up.

He's got three miles to walk before he gets home.

When he gets indoors, he's thinking to himself: "In two weeks' time my lad's going to be twelve. I want him down the pit with me."

So he goes through the front door, and there's a blazing coal fire. There's his missus and his lad in the kitchen, doing chores.

He says to his missus: "It's our lad's birthday in two weeks. He'll be twelve. I want him down the pit with me."

Well, an argument ensues between them. Of course, the man, at the time, loses the argument.

So he goes out on the back yard to calm down. And while he's on the back yard, the mother talks to her son.

She says: "You're not going down the pit with him. You know you're not. It doesn't matter what your father thinks.

"You can work on the farm and later on join the British Army. But one thing's for sure, you're not going down the pit.

"Just look at your father, his face pitted with coal. I wash his back and sooth his aching joints. By gum lad, you're not going down!

"Buried in the churchyard, there's lads no older than twelve. It's just a cavern of slaughter – a dark, deep, damp dungeon. That's all it is. If you want to be twelve my lad, you're not going down!"

Anyway, his dad gets his own way.

Two weeks later the lad goes down the pit for the very first time. This happens:

THE LAD

They brought him up the pit shaft
then took him from the cage.
His face was covered with coal dust,
they could not tell his age.
In fact, he was a young lad,
his first day down the pit.
He didn't hear the noises
before the wood prop split.
The roof came down and crushed him
against the stone hard floor
Squeezing out a young life
that would not laugh no more.
Who would tell his mother?
Who would tell his dad?
That coal has claimed another,
and this one just a lad.

4

5

6

7

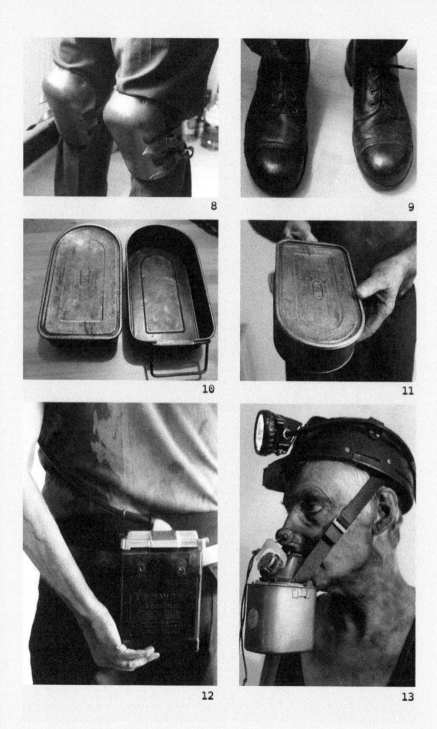

14

THE CLIFTON COLLIERY BAND.

15

Chapter 5

There are a couple of pictures of me at the start of the book, doing a bit of modelling. I'm demonstrating what a miner would have looked like between, say, 1950 and about 1970. I'm wearing all the equipment he would have carried.[2,3]

As I go through and talk about the various items, you can see photos showing in more detail what they're like.

I'll start with the helmet.[5] What is it made of, do you suppose? If I tap it, it makes a hollow, thumping noise. It's not made of plastic. It's not made of tin. It's not made of leather. It is made out of cardboard – compressed cardboard.

Basically, they are very good helmets. They are light in weight.

They are waterproof to a certain degree. But, being cardboard, what happens if you are working with water dripping on your head all the time?

It gets a bit mushy after a while and then it won't protect you. So you have to get another one.

Now, let's look at the lamp on the top of this miner's helmet.[6]

If you follow that cable, you can see it's attached to a battery on my belt. Now, how long do you suppose that battery will last? An hour? Two hours? Four hours?

It will last a lot longer than that. On full power, I would say twelve hours at least.

This is the main bulb in his lamp. It's very bright. Think of this – you're down the pit and your main bulb blows. It doesn't happen very often, but it can happen.

It's gone out. You're on your own. When your light goes out you cannot see the width of a piece of paper in front of your eyes. It is total blackness. So what are you going to do? No good shouting for your mam!

Well, the designers were very inventive.

They put in a second bulb.[7] The second bulb is what is called a 'pilot light'. It is not as powerful as the main light. But you can see just enough to get you out of trouble. That's all it's designed for.

These are knee pads.[8] Why do you think miners wear knee pads? It's because they work on their hands and knees all day, hewing coal.

And they have another use – you have to believe this. The miner comes home on a Friday night and wants to ask his missus if he can go down the pub. He knows he'll have to do a bit of grovelling. So he puts on his knee pads and gets down on his knees and says:

"Can I go down the pub, missus . . . please?"

Chapter 6

A miner's boots have steel toe caps across the front.[9] We're talking of 1950 here. If you dropped something metal on your toes it would protect them, if the thing you dropped is not too heavy. If it was something like a spanner, say.

If anything really heavy dropped on your toes these would be no good. The weight would just push the edge of the steel toe caps into your toes and chop them all off. So they were not much protection in 1950.

Everything down the pit is ultra-heavy. It has to be, especially if it's electrical, because it's got to be gas tight. I'll explain to you why.

If there's a fire or an explosion underground, you get a lot of carbon monoxide gas released.

You can't see carbon monoxide and you can't smell it, but it is highly toxic. If you breathe it in, it will kill you. Underground, with carbon monoxide in the air, if you haven't got a gas mask you haven't got a chance.

In September 1950, at Cresswell Colliery in north Derbyshire, there was an underground fire on a conveyor belt.

The men at Cresswell Colliery didn't have gas masks. They had no protection against the poisonous gas. On that day, eighty men were suffocated and died as a result of carbon monoxide poisoning.

So the Coal Board realised they needed to develop something to prevent similar accidents.

By 1960 the 'self-rescuer' gas mask had come into use. No man is allowed to go underground without one of these.[12]

The type of 'self-rescuer' shown in the photograph will last you for one hour only.[13]

In a fire or an explosion down the pit, you've got to be selfish. You do not sort out the casualties first. You've got to put on your 'self-rescuer' before you do anything else. If you don't, in a very short space of time, you will become a casualty yourself.

You've got a head strap, a mouthpiece and a nose clip.[14] Now, I want you to remember this. The only time you are allowed to take this off after an incident is when the Mines Rescue staff tell you.

Once you've got the mouthpiece in you cannot speak. The spit in your mouth makes a seal round the mouthpiece.

Right, let's imagine I can see smoke coming down the roadway and I'm on my own. I don't muck about. Helmet off, flip the red seal on the top of the 'self-rescuer' case and pull it out.

The head strap goes on first. Next, the mouthpiece, so I can't speak, and then nose clip. The sound I make, when I breathe with this on, is like Darth Vader! [15]

So, remember the question – when are you allowed to take this off? Right – when the Mines Rescue staff tell you.

There's only one other time you're allowed to take it off. That is when you see a beautiful lady down the pit and you want to give her a kiss!

Chapter 7

In the years between 1850 and 1913, how many men and boys do you think were killed down British coal mines? You may guess a hundred and fifty; five hundred; five thousand.

In fact, around ninety thousand men and boys were killed down British coal mines in that period.

The reason is the pit owners were ambitious. They wanted bigger profits so they started to go down deeper. But they didn't have the technology to do it safely.

There were a lot of hazards in the pits years ago. A man could be buried alive, drowned, gassed, electrocuted or blown up. As a miner would say – take your pick! There was no health and safety then.

Roof falls were the most common, when they only had wooden props to hold up the roof of the tunnels.

The weight of earth crushing down on those wooden props was massive. And the earth is not totally static. It moves and shifts ever so slightly. The wooden props sometimes collapsed under the strain and the roof came down.

The only good thing about wooden props was they used to 'talk to you'. As they shifted slightly, they made different sounds.

One sound said: "You're all right." But another sound said: "Get out quick!" because the roof was going to come down.

In early days of mining they never mapped where they put a shaft. A mine would be abandoned and then, over time, it would fill up with water.

Years later another coal mine would be sunk nearby. Without a map, the new miners would dig a tunnel and suddenly break through into an old, disused, unmarked shaft.

If that was brim full with water, of course, the water would just come pouring down the new tunnel and drown everybody who was working there.

In the infancy of electricity underground, in the early 1900's, it was cumbersome. It used to spark all over the place – and as you know yourself, sparks and gas don't mix.

Most miners wore hobnail boots down the pit, which had metal studs. They could cause sparks, too, that could lead to an explosion.

The men operating electrical equipment ended up wearing rubber boots instead of hobnails, and thick rubber gloves. They were not to keep their hands clean, but as insulation, for safety.

There was another hazard to electricity.

Now, something you have to realise about working underground – there are no facilities whatsoever for going to the toilet. If you want a wee, you have a wee, usually where you are standing.

In the infancy of electricity in the pits, often miners would have a wee and, without realising, they did it on a live cable and got electrocuted. A lot of men have been killed by not looking where they were having a wee.

Chapter 8

As mines were sunk to ever greater depths, it became more challenging to detect and control gas at these lower levels. Miners faced constant danger from asphyxiation, fires and explosions.

'Natural gas' occurs naturally in the ground. Its other name is methane. Methane and natural gas are one and the same thing. It is formed within the coal itself. It gets trapped there and can't escape. So when the miner comes along with his pick and shovel he releases the gas into the area where he is working.

Natural gas is lighter than air so it stays at roof level. You may walk into an invisible cloud of natural gas and get a mouthful. It makes you feel dizzy. You will fall down and possibly injure yourself.

But the good thing is that you fall down – the important word being 'down'. Fresh air is heavier than natural gas, so you fall down into fresh air. You get some breaths of fresh air and then you come round.

The worse thing about natural gas is that it's very, very explosive. It's the same gas as you have in your cooker at home. That's what causes most underground explosions.

Gas explosions were quite regular and years ago there was no such thing as stone dust in use.

When you get a gas explosion underground it will rush down the roadway because it explodes in a confined space. It is like a bullet being fired out of a gun. The bullet comes out and the gas follows it.

A pressure wave forms in front of the explosion which whips up the coal dust. The coal dust is made of very fine particles that you can't see. When that coal dust is whipped up, then of course that, in turn, explodes. A coal dust explosion is very violent.

As that pressure wave keeps going down the roadway, it whips up more coal dust in front of it, which keeps fuelling the explosion. It is a chain reaction that can cause the whole pit to blow up.

To try to counteract this chain reaction, in more recent times the use of stone dust was introduced. Basically it is crushed limestone, treated until it is so fine it looks like white flour.

The technique is to spread the stone dust everywhere. It is dusted onto the roof, the side walls of the roadway and especially on the floor.

The idea is that it will mix with the coal dust. The stone dust is heavier than the coal dust. So, if there is an explosion it prevents the coal dust being whipped up, therefore that chain reaction is stopped.

About 20 metres from the coal face, wooden barriers are placed about a metre from the top of the roof. These wooden barriers are laden with stone dust.

If there is an explosion at the coal face the pressure wave will knock the wooden barrier over and all the stone dust will then be air borne. It will mix with the coal dust to prevent further explosions. So you get the initial explosion but you won't get any more.

It has proved a very practical way of limiting the effect of underground explosions. Even if the men using it come out looking like snowmen!

Being in an explosion underground is even worse than being in an explosion above ground, for all the obvious reasons. You're in an enclosed space in the dark. Not something you want to think about.

The worst natural gas explosion was on 14 October 1913 at a colliery in South Wales. In that single blast four hundred and thirty-nine men and boys were killed.

It's a lot of people, isn't it? It took three months to give them all a burial service, there were so many. Terrible.

The name of the colliery is pronounced seng-HEN-ith. It is a Welsh name that is spelled Senghenydd.

Chapter 9

When I was a lad, mining was a job for life.
A man's father worked down the pit, and his father
worked down the pit, and his father worked down the
pit. So they followed in one another's footsteps.

By the time you were fourteen or fifteen you
got to know all about the pits anyway, because where
we lived, you could see the headstocks from the
house.

The miners spent all their time underground
getting the coal – and it's very dangerous – but then
they would talk about it after work. When the miners
were drinking, especially at the Miners' Welfare, that
was the conversation. Since you were a kid, the coal
seemed to be in your veins, and you knew you would
follow your father into the pit.

I was born in Eastwood, Nottinghamshire. I grew up in the local vicinity around Eastwood. I was the oldest of nine children. My father was the next to youngest in a family of twenty-two children.

I first went down the pit after leaving school. I started at the training centre at the age of 15 doing a lot of jobs and theory work on the pit top.

I worked in the stock yard where they kept the equipment. I worked with the surface joiners and the surface bricklayers. I loaded trucks up with mining supplies. I wasn't old enough yet to put them into the cage. An experienced man had to do that.

You couldn't go underground before the age of 16 and you had to be with an experienced man – like a mentor, you might say.

When I went underground I worked with a man called Billy. My job with him was going round collecting up equipment from around the mine to be re-used on other jobs.

Billy was a very experienced miner. He was 64 years old. He was about five foot tall. He'd got bow legs from working at a low coal face for so long.

He wasn't too fit, and me being a young whippersnapper tried to run him round the pit.

He'd say: "Hang on a bit!" and I had to slow down.

When you get a gang of miners having a break, having a bit of snap or something, the main topics of conversation, of course, were drinking and women.

Now, Billy was a lay preacher. If we were standing near a group of miners talking about those subjects, Billy would say, "Come on, David. Let's take you away from this. You don't want to hear about this at your age!" Whether I did want to or not!

He had to work at the mine until he was 65 years old – right until the last day.

After Billy retired I worked with other people. One job among many was collecting up metal pit props that had to be returned to the surface because they were being replaced.

Chapter 10

As I told you, I used to be in the Mines Rescue Service.[30]

There was a rigorous selection for the Mines Rescue Service. You had to have a minimum of two years working experience at the pit. It could be very physically demanding so you had to be extremely fit. Also, you had to be fully first-aid trained.

People did it out of commitment to their fellow miners. There was very little other reward. Certainly the pittance in extra pay was not an incentive.

Every new recruit began with an initial three weeks of intensive training. This covered every aspect of the job and looked at all the possible types of incidents you might have to attend.

When I was training, most accidents were machinery related rather than explosions or roof falls.

Eight times a year you had to go on a full scale training exercise. You had to be ready to respond to the real thing at a moment's notice, so you always had to be totally prepared.

We would be formed into teams and the first job was to appoint a team captain. When they asked for volunteers there was usually dead silence. No one came forward. So, as often as not, it would be me who put my hand up. Somebody had to, and I wanted to get on with the job in hand.

First of all, we would be taken to a pit that we were not familiar with. As likely as not, in the real situation you would find yourself somewhere you hadn't been before.

Then we would be given details of where the accident had happened, and a detailed map of the mine. We had to use the map-reading skills we had been taught to locate the incident.

Once we had sorted out where it was, we had to get ourselves there. Then the first job was to do a thorough exploration of the accident site.

We had to make a sketch map of the area, and mark on the map the position of any dead bodies we found.

On these training exercises they were live miners playing the part of dead bodies, but if it had been the real thing we may well have found people who had died.

All we did was mark the place where we found them. We left them there and moved on. There was nothing more to be done for them and there was a possibility we might find survivors that we could help. The bodies would be retrieved later.

Although it was a tough job, and of course often a very sad one, all those who volunteered felt it was very worthwhile.

An accident could happen to anyone – to your father or your brother or your best mate. Anyone might be glad of the Mines Rescue Service at some point.

And I know better than anyone how true that was. Because one day I had need of the Mines Rescue Service to come to my aid. The rescuer had to be rescued. But I will tell you about that later.

MINES RESCUE

Looking back, my face
turned black by sweat and dust,
Thoughts only for others,
in danger,
somewhere trapped.

They may be all right,
Or walled up in a tomb,
their lights becoming dimmer.
At the time, no one's sure.

In training, teamwork is all.
Endurance pushed.
Thoughts for others spur you on.

A sixth sense comes in handy.
Dangerous gas, falling rock,
show no mercy.

So why do it for a little extra pay?
Only I can answer that.

On the sixth of March 1991
the roles were reversed.
With thoughts only for others,
they came for me.

16

17

18

19

20

21

22

23

24

25

43

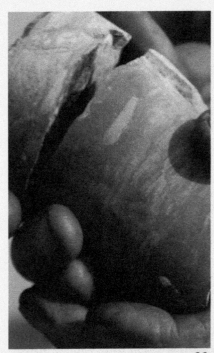

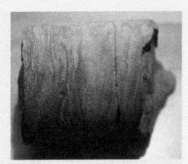

27

26

28

29

Chapter 11

Talking of accidents underground, wearing jewellery was one of the main causes of miners getting fingers ripped off. Working underground, if you got the band of a ring caught, your finger just got ripped off. Most miners were sensible and didn't do it.

If you wore a watch underground it had to be an old-fashioned wind-up one. It couldn't have a battery because of the danger of sparks that could lead to an explosion.

After a fire or an explosion down the pit, then you get a lot of carbon monoxide released. The slang for it is 'after-damp'. This comes from the German word 'dampf' meaning 'vapour'. So you could really say 'after-gas'.

I've explained to you about carbon monoxide and the 'self-rescuer'.

In the home, if you have a faulty boiler that leaks carbon monoxide, it can cause headaches, sickness, dizziness, stomach pains and difficulty breathing.

Occasionally, it can do more serious damage. If people block up the air vents in a room because they can feel a draft they could be in trouble. They could even die. You must have ventilation.

Ventilation down the pit is always an issue.

In the mines a supervisor is called a 'deputy'. A deputy carries a lamp that's not a lamp to see by. It's a lamp used for testing for methane gas. It's not an electric lamp. There's no bulb and no battery. It is an oil lamp.[16]

The lamp has a reservoir for fuel at the bottom, with a wick in it. The wick burns with a flame. There's a gadget that you use to control how big or small the flame is.

As I said, methane is lighter than air so it stays at roof level. To detect the gas, what you have to do first is turn the lamp flame down as low as possible.

Then position the lamp up high near the gas. Then let the gas come into the lamp.

If methane is present, a blue 'cap' will develop over the flame. The larger the blue cap, the more methane is present.

If you suspect there is a lack of oxygen, or carbon monoxide may be present, you hold the lamp down near the floor. If there is no oxygen or carbon dioxide is present the flame will go out.

This lamp is one hundred per cent fail-safe.

There is only one problem with these lamps. When you get them from the lamp cabin in the morning they are already lit. After quite a short time with the flame burning, they get hot.

Of course, when you've got it hanging on your belt, after a while it burns your leg.

So most men who have to carry one will shake it so the light goes out. That stops it getting hot.

But what are you going to do when you need to use it to test for gas? How can you relight it? You're not allowed to carry matches underground, so you can't strike a light.

There is a 'key' built into the lamp itself.[17]

It's a piece of metal about 7 cm long. You pull it out as far as it will go. Then you knock it in again hard with the heel of your hand[18], and it creates a spark within the lamp that relights the wick.

You can actually see it spark.[19] It works in a very similar way to a petrol cigarette lighter.

Chapter 12

Around 1920, in England, they had to mine at least 216 million tons of coal a year that was saleable.

216 million tons – that's a lot of coal, when you think about it. And all mined with a pick and shovel.

I'll break it down so that you can understand it better. In the 1920's there were very few coal-fired power stations. There were just a scattering around the country, that's all. So ten million tons of coal were used for power stations.

12 million tons of coal were used for powering steam trains. At that time there was no other source of power for trains. There were no electric trains and no diesels. Just steam.

The steam was produced by boiling water, using a coal fire. The locomotive was one big, mobile boiler.

A supply of coal and water was carried on the train, in a special compartment called a tender. The fireman had to spend the whole journey shovelling coal from the tender into the fire. He had to keep the water boiling because that was how the steam was generated. If they lost steam, the train would stop.

15 million tons of coal were used for steam ships. They worked on the same principle as trains. Men laboured round the clock to stoke the fires with coal to keep up steam pressure, to drive the ship's engines.

40 million tons of coal were for household use. 54 million tons were exported. 85 million tons went to industry, such as steel production.

The household use was to heat the home, to heat the water and to do the cooking.

Big stately homes had enormous kitchens and dozens of bedrooms. Each one had a coal fire. All the coal had to be brought to the room. The ashes had to be cleared away when the fire went out. It all created a lot of work for the servants.

In an ordinary home, the coal fire in the kitchen was the hub of the house.

GRANDMA'S OPEN FIRE

The fire keeps us warm in this small house,
The dog, the cat, the odd field mouse.
It boils the kettle, makes crispy toast.
The oven on the side cooks the Sunday roast.

It gets water for our tin bath really hot
And do you know something, missus,
There's some left over to wash my shirt.

It softens dripping for our bread,
But once a week
we have to clean it with black lead.

Oh, we owe a lot for coal and wood.
I'd be ten again only if I could.

The men would stand with their back to the fire, warming themselves – lovely! But in that era, men wore baggy trousers. They didn't feel the fabric in the folds getting hot. Then when they sat down they found the backs of their trousers were red hot and burned their legs and their backsides! They would jump up again quick and swear! I've seen it no end of times, and it always made me laugh.

Everybody had a coal fire in their house at that time. There were no alternative means of heating. Believe it or not, it was more beneficial in some ways than today's central heating. There were not so many coughs and colds when the house was not so warm.

For fire to burn, you have to have oxygen. When a coal fire was burning it was dragging oxygen from everywhere – under the door, round the window frames. For that fire to keep roaring away it needed a constant supply of oxygen.

You got fresh air, in the form of oxygen, circulating all around the house. The price you paid was feeling a draught as the air moved. Although it wasn't as comfortable, it kept you more healthy than the warm, stale air you get today with central heating.

Chapter 13

With a coal fire a lot of soot is produced inside the chimney. If you don't sweep the chimney every few months you get a build-up of soot and there is a danger it could catch fire.

Many a winter's night I've walked down a road of terraced houses and seen flames coming out of the chimney of one of them where the soot has caught fire.

To save the cost of a chimney sweep, you could get a set of rods and a brush and do it yourself.

I used to sweep our chimney. You started off with one rod. The brush was attached to this by screwing it on. You added more rods at the bottom, building up the height one rod at a time.

Altogether, the rods needed to be long enough to reach right to the top of the chimney and out of the top.

The brush was a flat wooden circle surrounded by bristles. It measured about 35cm across.[35] It had to be big enough to touch the chimney walls as it went up and down. There was a place to screw the first rod to the wooden centre-piece.

On one particular occasion things didn't go to plan. The brush had been out of the top of the chimney pot so the job was done. I pulled the rods down the chimney. I unscrewed them and took them off, one at a time, as I got them down.

For some reason, about halfway down, the brush came off and got stuck in the chimney. It was well and truly trapped up there. I couldn't get it down.

At the time we had a dog called Sandy. It was winter, and Sandy liked to stretch out in front of the open fire. It was a wonder she didn't burn herself, she got so close. She stood the heat and wouldn't shift.

So the next time the fire was lit, there was Sandy in her favourite place.

Remember, the brush was still stuck halfway up the chimney. The heat of the fire set light to it. It burned off the bristles and the blazing wooden centre-piece fell down the chimney into the burning coals.

That should have been the end of it – but no. It bounced off the coal, shot out of the grate and landed on our Sandy! I'd never seen a dog move so fast!

And I had to be quick to grab the red-hot lump of wood and chuck it back into the fire before it burned a hole in the carpet.

No damage was done to the dog or the carpet. But I got told off about that by my missus, in no uncertain terms, I can tell you.

Chapter 14

The coal fires everybody had in their houses produced large amounts of ash every day. Years ago the outside toilets used to be called 'ash pit' toilets.

People used to put ashes in the bottom of the toilet to soak up all the liquid and everything that went in. So a lot of the ashes went into the toilet. Once a week the 'night soil' men as they were called used to dig them out by hand with a shovel, put them into a cart and take them away. That was a smelly job!

People used to spread ash on the gardens as well, as a fertiliser, because there was potash in it.

If you were anything of a gardener, soot from the chimney was a prized commodity. You couldn't use it straight away because it had too many chemicals in it. You had to leave it for about six months to mature. Then it was full of nutrients for the soil. To anybody who used to grow things, it was gold dust, soot was.

They used to put it on the soil at the end of the year and let it soak in over the winter.

We talk about recycling today but years ago everything was recycled. It was easier in those days because there were very few synthetic materials, so everything would rot down.

Nothing was wasted in those days. If you were a poor family you had to think of your waste products and how you could use them. Everything was used. All the waste from preparing vegetables went on to a compost heap or to feed livestock.

A lot of people used to keep chickens. When they were ready for the pot, the chickens would be killed and the feathers plucked off them. Then they would be roasted or put in a stew. And a use would be found for the feathers too, filling a cushion.

My dad had hutches full of tame rabbits for eating. If we were short of meat he'd go out to the hutch and pick out the biggest one. Then, chop! He'd skin it right away and it was in the pan before it was cold.

People needed to supplement their diet as cheaply as possible. And they were not squeamish about killing and preparing their food to eat. It's only in relatively recent times that meat has come pre-packaged and ready prepared. Poorer people, especially in country areas, always did it themselves.

It was quite common for people to keep a pig – just the one. It was fed on kitchen waste. The family would fatten it up, usually until Christmas. Then they would take it to the slaughterhouse. The slaughter man would do his business. He would be paid with a cut of meat for doing it, not paid with money.

In my grandmother's house there was no fridge or anything like that. There was a cold room with a granite slab. It was chilly in there, even in summer. My grandma used to have hams hanging up in there that she had cured herself, and bacon. It would keep for months. That was how they preserved things in those days.

Chapter 15

Going back to lamps, I also have a different type of lamp from the one I talked about before. This is not a safety lamp. This particular lamp is very special to me. It was my granddad's personal lamp.[20,]

This was the lamp he used to see with down the pit. It's an oil lamp.[21] His lamp was number 678.[23]

If he knocked the light out, he'd had it. You couldn't relight these type of lamps. Most miners used to carry two of them so they always had one in reserve.

Despite the danger, men did used to sneak cigarettes down the pit with them years ago. But if you did sneak a fag down, you couldn't light your fag with a lamp like this one.

There is actually a place to put a padlock on the lamp, so you can't unlock it.[22]

Usually, when you went down the pit, you could expect to be searched by the banksman.

He's the man in charge of emptying and refilling the cages that go up and down the shaft. He would pull a man out at random and check him.

He would search him to make sure he had no contraband on him, such as matches. Taking anything like that down was a serious offence because you were putting hundreds of lives at risk.

But complacency is just as big a hazard to life and limb when you are working in such dangerous conditions.

I'll give you an example of what happened to me, when I was a young lad.

There was one particular chap I worked with who expected me to do everything I was told without question. If I didn't, he would get angry.

So I did whatever he said.

On one occasion he decided we should jump on the conveyor belt to go up this roadway. It was illegal for men to ride on the conveyor, but that didn't deter him.

He was sure we wouldn't get caught. Complacency on his part. So, on we jumped.

We didn't know at the time, but at the top of this roadway there were very bad roof conditions.

Explosives had been put in place to blow it all down so they could put new roof supports in.

But we were travelling up on the conveyor belt at the time.

Now, they were in the wrong for putting explosives in the roof, because that is where gas is found. That is where their complacency comes in.

But they had done it before and got away with it, so they thought they could get away with it again.

Also, they should also have sent someone down to stop people coming up the roadway where they had set explosives. But they didn't.

They didn't expect anybody coming that way. Complacency again.

And they should have stopped the conveyor belt, as well. But they didn't bother.

Complacency.

Well, when we got near . . . BOOM! What an explosion. You couldn't see for dust. We were nearly underneath it.

Luckily, neither of us got hurt.

But nobody dared say anything. We were in the wrong for being on the conveyor, and those other chaps were in the wrong too.

But you see how easily complacency nearly caused a disaster.

30

31

32

33

34

35

36

37

Chapter 16

Let's turn to a happier topic. What I'm going to tell you about now are 'snap' tins.[10,11] I wonder if you know what those are? And why they're called snap tins?

I expect you'll say: "It's because you keep your snap in them!" You're right, but only half right.

I think the real reason they are called that is because in Victorian times there was a small cottage industry in South Wales that used to make these tins for the miners. And that company was called 'Snap'.

So, any food a miner puts in it is called his 'snap'. He doesn't say his lunch, or his sandwiches. He says his snap.

The tin is a rather unusual shape. One end is rounded and one end square. That is because years ago, when everyone used to do their own baking, they always used to make a two pound loaf for the family.

The top end was rounded and the bottom end was square. So when they cut a slice off the loaf, it fitted exactly into the snap tin. That's the reason for that shape.

You put your bread and dripping or your bread and jam in one half and you put the other half over it, like a lid, and they just hold together. There's a loop for you to carry it on your belt.

You need to keep all food safely covered in a metal box down the pit, because of what lives down there in the dark.

Now I'm going to tell you a true story about a snap tin.

You can't work at the coal face until you are 18 years old, when you start your training.

We had a young lad with us, just 18, and we were training him.

When you sit down to eat your snap together down the pit, you each turn your main light off because otherwise you would blind each other, all those bright lights so close.

Now, this young fellow had false teeth at the front. I think he'd been scrapping and got them knocked out. So when he was ready for his snap, he took out his false teeth and put them in the snap tin instead of his sandwich. That way he'd easily be able to find them when he'd finished his meal.

After about five minutes eating his food he could hear a scratching and scraping noise coming from his tin. So he switched his light on and there were a couple of mice in his snap tin, making off with his teeth.

They had got them over the edge of the tin and were dragging them away. So do you know what he did? He snatched at this mouse and tried to grab his teeth. But the mouse held on. He had a right tussle with it to get his teeth back.

When he got them, he wiped them on his dirty shirt, all covered in coal dust, and put them back in!

"I've got a date tonight," he said, "so I've got to have my teeth back. I'll make sure they're not where the mice can get to them again!"

Chapter 17

The job I did in the pit was mine ventilation.
I worked on two coal faces and several development
areas where new coal faces were being opened up.

I found, down the pit, you use every sense you
were born with.

I was working in the same part of the pit a lot
of the time, so I got to know the smell of the area. If
the smell was different one day you knew there was
something wrong.

You are under artificial light that your eyes get
adjusted to, and sometimes you would see things you
wouldn't normally see. I was working on my own and
I was so used to being around the same areas that
I would notice things.

I found that my hearing was more acute.
I would listen out for things and be aware of anything
unusual.

If I was going up a roadway I would touch the
side of the roadway where the metal roof supports
were. If they were warmer than normal, I would know
there might be something brewing. There could be
a fire starting somewhere. Sometimes a fire would
start in a waste area and you would get 'sweating' –
like beads of moisture – on the roof supports.

The 'deputy' is in charge of the coal face
workmen and their safety but he couldn't do
everything. He might not spot these things because he
is too busy with the men on the coal face.

But me, checking all these areas every day,
I could sense when something was not right. I could
anticipate. Sometimes I could sense things before the
electrical equipment picked them up. Then I could
alert the deputy.

Part of my job was to regularly test the
monitoring equipment that was installed underground
to detect gas. You have to remember that mechanical
equipment will only do what it is designed to do. It
hasn't got a mind. It can't think.

I used to wander around with two bottles in a holder I carried over my shoulder. One was full of carbon monoxide and the other methane gas.

What I had to do was 'gas' the monitors to see if they were working right. First of all, I had to ring the pit top to tell them I was going to 'gas' a certain monitor, so they knew it was a test, not an actual incident.

I would ask them to tell me the reading they had, and then I would 'gas' the piece of equipment, and then get a second reading. Sometimes I had to recalibrate the monitor according to the results.

Then I would go half a mile down the roadway and do the next one. And so on, and so on.

Walking these roadways every day, and looking at them so closely, I did find something unusual on a couple of occasions. Nothing dangerous – actually something rather beautiful. I found fossil ferns in the rock wall of the roadway.[25 & 25]

I also have a piece of a trial boring that had been made at the pit. It is a smooth length of solid rock.[26,27,28,29] But the rock split, and there inside was a fossil of a plant that had not seen the light of day for millions of years. Magical.

Chapter 18

Now, the next bit of equipment I'm going to tell you about is called an 'air sampler'.[36] These are taken down the pit once a week, on a regular basis, to take an air sample where you are working to make sure it is fit to breathe.

In a rescue situation one of the Mines Rescue men would take one of these down, with his rescue gear on. Up above, at the top of the pit, if there was an emergency they would bring a portable laboratory to analyse the sample as quickly as possible.

This is a pump – a bit like a bicycle pump – but it works in reverse. Instead of blowing air out, it sucks it in.

All you do is fix one of these tubes into it.[36]

Then, before you can use it, you have to give it about twenty pumps to clear it. This is in case there is any contaminated air already inside it.[37]

It is a modern luxury to be able to analyse the air scientifically to make sure it is safe to breathe after an explosion. It has saved countless lives.

After a fire or an explosion you get a lot of carbon monoxide produced. You can't see it or smell it. In years gone by, in the early 1900's before the rescue service was formed, they would go down the pit on a rescue and, of course, the rescuers got gassed themselves.

Someone had the idea of using a warm-blooded animal to test ahead for gas. They thought about mice but they were not suitable because they run about. A canary, though, will sit still on its perch, so that's what was chosen.

They would take a canary down in a cage, and hold it in front of them when they went into the area where they suspected there was gas.[38] If the canary fell off its perch, gassed, the rescuers would back off. Even up until the 1990's canaries were still used by the Mines Rescue as a back-up.

Although it was a Victorian idea, it never let you down. If for some reason the electrical equipment didn't work, there was a fail-safe with the canary. On any rescue they went on they always took canaries in cages and kept them in fresh air, just in case.

In more recent times a small bird size recovery container was invented, complete with tiny oxygen cylinder, so that if a canary was gassed on a rescue mission it was possible to revive it.[39]

As a tribute to the canary, every pit top, near the manager's office usually, had an aviary full of canaries. Although they didn't use them much, they still kept them – not to use, but as a tradition. There was always somebody nominated to look after them. They saved many, many lives.

In Victorian times, if there was an explosion near the pit bottom, before the miners would go down they would put a dog in a harness and lower it down. They would leave it at the bottom for a little while then pull it back up. If the dog was alive the men would go down, but not otherwise.

Sometimes people feel quite revolted by the use of animals to detect gas in the pit, but they saved lives. In earlier times they didn't have anything else.

Chapter 19

Most people working down the pit end up with a nickname. My nickname was "Dry Bread". The way I got that nickname was this.

Me and my dad worked at the same pit and had the same shift. My mum always packed up our snap in paper overnight and put it out on the table.

One day she had six slices of dry bread left on the end of her loaf. She put them in paper and not thinking, she put them down on the table with our snap. Next morning, me, going to work in a hurry, I grabbed the wrong paper package. When it came to snap time, I took out six slices of dry bread!

They got on to my father something rotten. "Fancy sending your lad down the pit with dry bread!" The deputy said straight away: "Dry Bread – that's

what we're going to call you from now on." They
never let us forget it.

I spend a lot of time giving talks to people
about life down the pit. I dress up like a miner, the
way I am in the photographs in this book.[1,2,3] I tell
the audience the kind of things that I've been telling
you here. I show them the equipment we used and
demonstrate how it works.

It's something I really enjoy doing. I don't take
a fee for these talks. Any money the organisers
collect at the door is all donated to charity.

I'm involved with a lot of voluntary work,
helping the community in one way or another. It's very
important to me.[47]

I had an interesting experience a few years ago
when a play was put on in New York. It was called
"The Daughter-in-Law" by D.H. Lawrence.

The play is set in the early years of the
20th century in a mining community in Eastwood, in
Nottinghamshire. Well, that's where I come from, so
I reckon I should know a bit about it.

The producers got the dress right, they got
the acting right, but what couldn't they do? They
couldn't do the local lingo could they! The local accent

defeated them. So the producers in New York asked me to demonstrate the accent to them.

I did this by means of a series of transatlantic phone calls. I did my best D.H. Lawrence accent (tha' knors!) They would record my voice for the actors who then had to learn and try and copy my accent.

I told them some of our local sayings too. I told them what a 'clart-fart' is. Do you know what that is? It's a gossip! Do you know any clart-farts? I bet you do! Quite a few! Don't mention any names!

The BBC rang me up to discuss doing a broadcast for Radio 4. It never came to anything, but I was on stand-by to go down to London for a programme.

They mentioned that in their archives they had sound recordings from the 1930's. They had the noise of men riding up and down the pit shaft and of a man working at the coal face with a pick and shovel.

The BBC copied these recordings for me so that when I go out to do a talk, people can hear what actual working life was like underground back in those days.

Chapter 20

Do you know what other animals used to help men down the pit? Horses. In the past they used donkeys, or asses, but mainly they used small Shetland-type ponies.

The pony, if it went into a low area, had to wear a special horse helmet.[32,33] The helmet is made of very tough leather. If he didn't have it on, he could rip his head to pieces on the roof.

Horses were equipped with helmets down the pit before men were, believe it or not.

Pit ponies all had names and they all had personalities. They were inspected every day to make sure they had no injuries and their feet were in good order. They could not work if they lost a shoe.

There were blacksmiths based at the pit top to make horseshoes.[40,41] They were provided with a forge and an anvil. But of course, because of the ever-present danger of gas, they couldn't take them underground.

They had to make the horseshoes in their smithy, but then take them down the pit and nail them on to the ponies' hooves cold.

This wasn't a very comfortable procedure for the ponies and some of them played up. Back in Victorian times, when they did that, or if a pony was very stubborn, they used the twitch.[34]

They put the loop of the twitch under the pony's bottom lip and twisted it. Eventually it would hurt, so the pony would stop misbehaving and do what it is was told. That practice stopped in more modern times.

The ponies were well looked after and well fed. Every day, on their way back to their under-ground stables, the ponies were driven through a bath of water and scrubbed clean with a broom.

Before they went in they looked all alike – all black. When they came out, you could tell them apart again.

Often, young lads looked after the ponies and got very fond of them.[48]

THINKING BACK

My name is Ben.
I was only thirteen
Working underground at Moorgreen pit
With Sonny, my pony.

I treated him well.
He'd do anything for me.
Sonny had a nose bag
But he would still pinch my snap.

Scars on his back,
Low roofs are to blame.
Scars of my own,
but at least I went home.

No green fields,
Only black dusty roads.
Poor Sonny
He's past his best.

Heavy work wore him out.
The vet came.
Sonny knew why.
They put him down.
A tear trickles, thinking back.

I came across a woman from London who took exception to the use of pit ponies. She said it was cruel to use horses underground. But before that, it was women and children who dragged the loaded coal carts to the bottom of the pit shaft. So using ponies was seen as a step forward and more humane.

At that time, everything was horse-drawn everywhere. Above ground, in many places steam power took over from horses, but you couldn't use steam power underground because of the dangers of explosions.

Neither could you use motor vehicles because they need petrol, and that is too dangerous to take down the pit. So horses provided a very necessary function without potentially endangering life.

Jim was the last pit pony to come up out of Moorgreen pit in about 1973. You can see from his picture what a little horse he was, compared with the two big ones alongside him.[42] The horse helmet in the previous pictures was Jim's helmet.[31,32]

38

39

40

41

43

42

44

Chapter 21

By 1950 the ponies were not the only ones getting a bath after their shift. Pit head baths started to come into use for the men.

Can you believe, it was another ten years before all collieries had them.

They were a revolution. Before the baths were introduced, miners had always had to walk home covered in black coal dust and muck from the pit.

Usually they came into a house with no hot water, no central heating and no bathroom. So how did they cope?

The mother shoo'd the children out of the way while the man of the house stripped off his filthy pit clothes. He took his bath in a tin tub in front of the coal-fired kitchen range. And another regular job for the miner's missus was to scrub his back.

The water was heated on the range. That was the same range where mother boiled the kettle, cooked the dinner, and dried the washing.

The heart of the home, it was.

When my dad was a young kid, he told me he kept a hedgehog as a pet. They had a big fire guard round the kitchen range and the hedgehog lived in there. It never used to hibernate. It lived in the fire range for years.

Anyway, when the bathtub was not in use, it was kept hanging on a nail outside in the yard.

So you can imagine what a luxury it was when pit head baths were provided. It was a boon to be able to have a hot shower before going home.

I have a tablet of soap that is original soap from the 1950's. It has 'PHB' stamped on it, which stands for 'pit head baths'. It was pure carbolic.[31]

The only problem was, when you have a shower, you can clean yourself front and sideways, but you can't clean your back.

So you're in the shower and you turn to the chap next to you and say: "Give my back a wash, will you, mate?"

So he'd wipe a sponge across your back. And then he'd ask the next man to do the same for him. And so on, and so on. I've seen as many as ten men, all in one line, each washing somebody's back.

And then the man at the front of the line has to run round and wash the back of the man at the end.

They looked like so many elephants walking round a circus ring, except they weren't holding each other's tail!

Chapter 22

A lot of miners were keen gardeners. They spent their free time cultivating their garden or their allotment.

Fruit and vegetable shows were very popular. There were always a lot of people entering their produce, hoping to win a prize for the best carrots or the best cabbages or whatever. There was a lot of rivalry.

Unfortunately, if the same grower kept winning all the time, some jealous person might try a bit of sabotage. They shouldn't have done it, but they did.

But the owners were savvy. They kept careful watch on their prize produce and made sure no one got near it to do anything to spoil it.

In the north-east of England they were renowned for growing large leeks. No one else could compete with the size of them. Each man had his own personal recipe for fertiliser and he guarded it from everyone. A certain Mr Taylor of County Durham was a prize winner in 1955.[46]

Near us there were big local agricultural and horticultural shows where people came from all around with livestock and other produce. There was always a big marquee full of flowers and fruit and vegetables. They looked magnificent.

There were sections for preserves and cakes and bread, too.

I first started baking bread when I was a young lad. It wasn't successful at all. I dropped some on the floor and it was that bad even the dog wouldn't go near it. So my grandma said: "You'd best come round to my house."

So I went round to my grandma's house and she showed me how to make bread the old-fashioned way. I got really good at it so I thought: "Right – I'll give it a try." I entered the bread making class at the annual show. I was the only man amongst all the local women. And I got first, second and third prize!

I kept the prize cards and I've still got them.[43]

BREAD, TEA AND ROSES

Sharpened pick blades attack the coal
with a vexed, hostile force.
This primitive, brutal work.

Heaped tubs of shattered coal
pushed by tin-ribbed lads.
They've no choice to be down here.
Pressed into men before their time.

Our rough-cut humour,
Loud passing of wind,
The reek of last night's ale.
Walking home past 'The Three Tuns' pub
With its dingy windows
and gas-lit rooms.

Our grinding pit boots on cobbled streets.
Laughter-creased faces show ivory teeth.
The scent of sweat on raggy clothes.
Thread-bare caps on dusty hair.

Before a wash
I'll sit in my garden
with a cup of tea,
Amongst my roses
and the waft of baking bread.

Chapter 23

Another thing that was a big pastime was keeping racing pigeons. (I don't race pigeons any more because they kept beating me!)

Whippet racing was a big sport too. Not just here, but all over. When I was a kid I used to go just below Eastwood, to a place called "The Breach". There was a playing field where they used to train whippets to race.

Two men would work together on the race. The track would be about a hundred yards long. They would concoct a contraption made from an up-turned bicycle and a length of rope.

They left the back wheel on the bike but instead of a tyre they rigged up a long loop of rope. This went round a post of some sort at the other end of the track.

Whippets love to chase, so the rope would have a piece of rag tied on it to act as a lure to get the dogs running.

One man would stand at one end of the race track and one at the other end. The first man started pedalling the bike like mad with his hands. This would pull the rope along the track at great speed.

When the rag got to a certain point, the other man let the whippets go. Away they would dash after the lure!

Also, right or wrong, whippets were used for poaching. They were after rabbits. The men used to go poaching anywhere they shouldn't!

My dad had a greyhound. He lived in the countryside and he was a bit of a poacher. Whippets are small and fast and more agile than a greyhound.

Miners were poor, and they had a lot of children. They went poaching to supplement what little meat they could afford to buy.

Years ago, all the men and boys walked to work at the pit.

It didn't matter if it was sunny and bright, or winter, rain or snow – you walked it.

WALKING TO WORK

As the crisp dawn air nips my ears,
I'll be glad when I'm down the pit.

Dusty and dangerous, maybe,
but at least it's warm.

The dip in the field
where icy mist hangs around
like the smoke from a bonfire
on a windless day.

My second-hand coat
With a missing button or two,
I'm very grateful.

Wearing well-worn hobnail boots
With dubbin-filled leathery cracks.
They keep out the wet.
My toes are numb
But my feet are dry.

Five minutes and I'll be there
Among danger and dust
But – at least it's warm.

Sometimes they would set a rabbit snare on their way to work, and on the way back pick up the dead rabbits. A man had to be sure no one knew where his snares were, or they would be taking his rabbits before he got to them.

Rabbits belonged to the landowner, but they were not really of any value to him. In fact, they were a nuisance. But still the landowner didn't want people going over his land and taking what didn't belong to them.

Gamekeepers were not interested in protecting rabbits, but if the landowner knew they turned a blind eye, they could be in trouble.

There was unofficial taking of fish, too. In fact, I was guilty of that, when I was a lad.

We used to go fishing with a bit of line in your hand, a hook and a home-made float my dad had made. We caught loads of fish. Perch and roach were quite good eating.

My grandma showed me how to clean and gut them. Then she soaked them in salt water overnight and next day we had roach and perch for dinner. It was brilliant.

Chapter 24

On their time off, most of the men went to the Miners' Welfare or the pub. It wasn't just for the drinking. Pubs, years ago, were a meeting place. It was a social gathering.

They had darts teams, dominos, crib. There was always a snooker table at the Miners' Welfare. So there were a lot of activities going on. Much later, of course, they had a television to watch the sport.

My dad was a good darts player. He was only five foot four. Actually, that's an exaggeration. His army pay book says he was five foot three and three-eighths.

There's a picture of him, all dressed up, with this pipe and a pint, at the Miners' Welfare.[45]

On this particular occasion he was in the darts team and he was taking part in a tournament. This bloke on the visiting team comes up to him.

My dad being only five foot four, the chap's a bit cheeky with him and says: "I'll go outside and get a brick for you to stand on, mate."

Never one to refuse a challenge, my dad says: "All right. Go and fetch me one then."

So he did. And my dad stood on it and he threw and got double top – bang! He won the match outright. If he hadn't stood on this brick he could only have reached double nineteen. So the bloke wished he'd never spoken.

They were quite talented people, miners, many of them. A lot of them had musical aspirations. Some were singers or played instruments. Brass bands were very popular and so were choirs.

It was in Northumberland, I think, there was a group of miners who were very interested in art. They arranged to have some classes in painting and they really took to it. This was in the 1930's but it continued for a lot of years.

They painted what was all around them. Their subjects were very much the subjects that I've talked about in this book. They painted their working lives, their workmates, the pit ponies, the equipment they used. And they painted their leisure activities, too. There are the whippets and the game of dominos, the pigeon lofts and even the poaching!

They became very famous, and a play was written about them called "The Pitman Painters".

We didn't have anything organised like that in our area, but we had a lot of people who were keen on music.

Choirs and brass bands didn't just play in front of a small local audience. They took part in big social events, too, like the annual galas.

The whole town was taken over for the gala, with marquees and stages and hundreds of people marching through the streets, with music and entertainment.

The Durham Miners' Gala is still an annual event today. It has been going for more than 120 years. It carries on as a tribute to the industry that used to be so fundamental to the way of life in that area.

A lot of the pits in Nottinghamshire had a brass band.[15] Many of them were prize winners in regional and national competitions. Although the collieries have gone, the tradition of the bands continues with local players from the area. Women play in them now, alongside the men.

Practically every pit had a male voice choir too. The quality of the singing was just beautiful. I was never a singer myself.

Over our way, at Annesley, around the early 1900's, there was one miners' choir in particular called "The Top Hat Club".

There's a photograph of them all dressed up in top hats and tails.[48]

All of them had the most luxuriant moustaches. That must have been one of the rules of joining, I think! There was only one young chap that didn't. He must have not yet been a full member.

There is only one not wearing a top hat. He was the pianist and he wore a bowler.

There was no sickness benefit or anything like that in those days. So what "The Top Hat Club" did was sing benefit concerts for miners who, for whatever reason, couldn't work and were pressed for money.

45

46

47

48

Chapter 25

Now, I promised you I would tell you something about my needing to call on the Mines Rescue Service as a customer rather than as a rescuer.

But first of all, you need to know something about cable cars, so I will explain.

If you think of cable cars, you probably think of ski lifts going up to the top of a mountain. But there are other types.

Years ago they were used to operate street tramways on steep hills. There is a famous cable car still running in San Francisco.

The cars' wheels run on rails but they don't run under their own power. The cars are attached to a moving cable that drags them up the hill.

All cable cars have two things in common. One is that they are suitable for operating on slopes. The other is the principle on which they work.

At either end of the slope there is a large revolving wheel. Each wheel has a groove round the outside.

A continuous loop of steel cable stretches between the two wheels and fits into the groove.

The wheel at the top is powered by a motor that turns the wheel.

The cars are fastened onto the steel cable with special bolts.

When the motor is switched on, the top wheel turns and moves the cable. As the cable moves, the cars go with it.

The cable takes cars up on one side and down on the other.

The cars move at the same speed, because they are pulled along by the same cable. If they start together, as one arrives at the top the other arrives at the bottom.

The cable is then stopped and the cars can be detached.

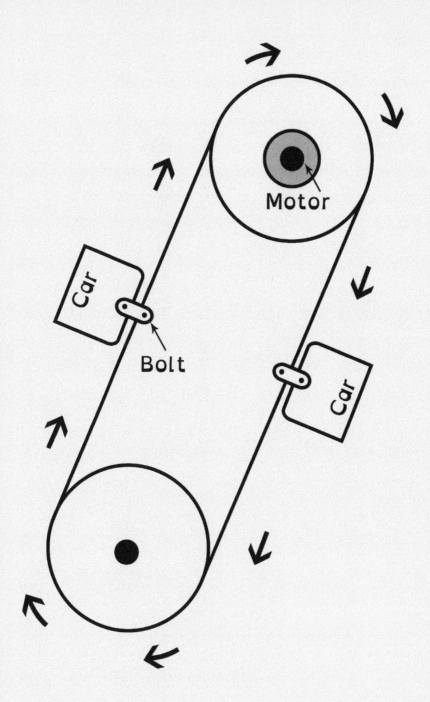

Motor

Bolt

Car

Car

Cable cars were also used in coal mines to run underground railways along sloping tunnels.

Heavy equipment often had to be moved around the mine and delivered to a new site. Waste material needed to be taken to the pit shaft to go above ground for disposal. Men were carried through the tunnel system to their place of work or to carry out inspections and repairs.

In the confined space of an underground tunnel, the cable railway operated as a single track with a passing point. There was a pre-arranged system of signals for the cable to stop and start during its journey. The speed limit was strictly controlled.

Different types of transportation were used depending on the purpose of the journey. For example passenger cars, flat-bed transporters or goods wagons.

There was a station at the top of the run and another at the bottom. Here, the various vehicles could be fastened on to the cable or detached from it.

Chapter 26

On this particular day I had finished my shift and gone home. I was just sitting down to a nice chicken dinner when the phone rang. I was needed back at the pit immediately. There was a dangerous situation with gas. Extra emergency ventilation was needed.

Without it, it was likely that production would have to be stopped and everybody evacuated. That was bad news because it meant a huge loss of earnings of course.

So I rushed back to the pit and joined my fellow ventilation engineer and we got to work. The underground mine workings cover miles. We had a lot to do, measuring and checking. Bit by bit, we made sure the whole place was properly ventilated and gas was no longer a hazard.

At 3 o'clock in the morning we had about done. Of course, it never gets light down the pit, but you still know when you've done a long shift.

We just needed to get to the top of the particular tunnel we were in and we could go up to the surface. The distance was about three-quarters of a mile. It was a sloping tunnel with an average gradient 1:12, so quite a steep slope. It was served by a cable railway.

We requested permission to ride up, which was granted. It was a three car train. We were the only ones aboard and we were in the back car. We were pleased to sit down for a little while.

At the passing loop we waved to a group of men going down in a passenger car, escorting a large piece of equipment on a flat-bed transporter they were taking down to the bottom to be relocated.

What happened next is a complete blank in my memory, but apparently the story went something like this.

At the top of the tunnel there were two goods wagons fastened together, waiting for the next transport down. They were each fully loaded with heavy 2-meter-long steel posts.

For some reason these two goods wagons moved. Being on a slope, once they started to go, with the weight of them, they didn't stop.

They ran away down the hill and a few minutes later smashed headlong into our passenger car coming up. Someone estimated they were going at about 70 mph.

Chapter 27

An accident like that on the motorway would be bad enough, but can you imagine it in the confined space of an underground tunnel? What wasn't ripped apart was squashed flat.

The top layer of steel posts shot out of the runaway wagons and hurtled down the tunnel like javelins! Anyone in the front car would have been killed, without question.

My mate was thrown out of his seat. He was not severely hurt, fortunately. He was first on the scene to try to rescue me. The others came up the tunnel as fast as they could to help.

My legs were trapped under the seat. I was folded up double, and the carriage roof and side panels were crushed down on top of me.

They couldn't move the panels off me because one of the runaway goods wagons had reared up and come to rest on top of the car I was in. Before they could shift it they had to unload what was left of the steel posts, to take some of the weight off it.

The tunnel was full of debris. There was nowhere safe to climb or stand, or stack the steel posts. But they tackled it.

When they were finally able to get at the panels, it took three men to pull them off me. First they got my head and shoulders out, and then gradually the rest of me.

I'm told that while this was being done I stopped breathing and had to be resuscitated with mouth-to-mouth and heart massage.

Somebody had fetched an emergency stretcher and they laid me on that. They strapped me on to it because now they had to climb with it over the debris of the wrecked train to get me up to the top of the tunnel.

The Mines Rescue Service had been called out, but by the time they arrived my workmates had got me out and on the way to safety. I was told later that I stopped breathing again in the ambulance on the way to hospital and had to be revived again.

I'm very thankful that I don't remember anything about it. In fact, I knew nothing about what had happened until I woke up in hospital ten days later.

I had a terrifying catalogue of injuries. I had a fractured skull. The fracture was right across the front of my head. My neck was severely injured. I had eight broken ribs down the left side. I had a collapsed right lung. One of my ribs had punctured my liver.

My right leg was injured below the knee. My left leg was dislocated at the hip. My left hip was fractured and when my leg dislocated, the side of my hip was taken clean off. There was nothing left to hold my leg together. My left arm was paralysed. My right shoulder was injured.

I had died twice and been resuscitated twice. They suspected brain damage. They told my wife that I'd never make it – I'd got too many injuries.

So when I woke up in that hospital bed some people thought I'd have been better off dead than alive.

But there's one person who wouldn't agree with that – ME!

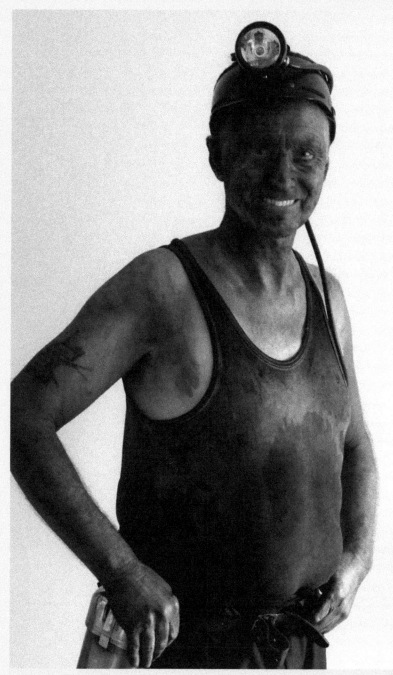

49

List of Photographs

When a photograph is mentioned in the text,
a small identifying number is printed beside it.

ACKNOWLEDGEMENTS

Warm acknowledgement and many thanks to Ian Winstanley for permission to use his poem "The Lad" on page 17. (All other poems by the author)

Photographs - many thanks and acknowledgements to:

Gavin Holman and IBEW (Internet Bandsman's Everything Within) for permission to use the photograph of Clifton Colliery Prize Band on page 20.

Robert Bradley (Healey's Heroes) for permission to use the photograph of a canary in use underground and the canary recovery box, both on page 83.

Beamish Museum for permission to use the photograph of Mr Taylor with his giant leeks on page 101.

Stephen Wainwright (Sutton Beauty & Heritage) for the photograph of the head gear on the front cover.

Jeff Vyse for the photograph on the back cover.

If you would like to hear The Pitman's voice reading the poems in this book, in his distinctive Eastwood accent, there is a way to do this on the web site:

www.dayglobooks.co.uk

You may be interested to know about

The National Coal Mining Museum for England
Caphouse Colliery
New Road
Overton
Wakefield
WF4 4RH

Tel: 01924 848 806
Email: info@ncm.org.uk

Underground tours available daily.

Lightning Source UK Ltd.
Milton Keynes UK
UKHW020231260919
350442UK00008B/53/P